365 GOOD HEALTH HINTS

365 GOOD HEALTH HINTS

Dr. David J. Pine

Hay House, Inc.
Carson, CA

Published and distributed in the United States by:
Hay House, Inc., 1154 E. Dominguez St., P.O. Box 6204, Carson, California 90749-6204

Edited by: Jill Kramer
Typesetting/internal design by: Freedmen's Typesetting Organization, Los Angeles, CA

The author of this book does not dispense medical advice nor prescribe the use of any technique as a form of treatment for physical or medical problems without the advice of a physician, either directly or indirectly. The intent of the author is only to offer information of a general nature to help you in your quest for physical fitness and good health. In the event you use any of the information in this book for yourself, which is your constitutional right, the author and the publisher assume no responsibility for your actions.

Library of Congress Cataloging-in-publication Data

Pine, David.
    365 good health hints / David J. Pine.
        p.   cm.
    ISBN 1-56170-099-1 : $5.95
    1. Self-care, Health. 2. Medicine, Preventive. I. Title. II. Title: Three hundred and sixty-five good
health hints. III. Title: Three hundred sixty-five good health hints.
RA776.95.P56   1994   94-16934
613—dc20   CIP

ISBN 1-56170-099-1

99 98 97 96 95   5 4 3 2 1
First Printing, August 1994

Printed in the United States of America on recycled paper

Preface

　　Being a chiropractic physician, my primary goal for my patients is not just to help them get well, but to help them stay healthy. That is the purpose of this book: to give you, the reader, sensible hints for maintaining good health. One can find health hints by reading a variety of different publications, but this book gives you the opportunity to access easy-to-follow advice in one all-inclusive source.

　　It is not my intention to give hardcore medical information, but simply to guide you on how to get the most out of life. The book covers topics such as how to care for your body, proper diet, different forms of exercise, and more. However, one cannot change his or her lifestyle overnight, so after you have read through this book, pick it up frequently to refresh your memory and to make these health hints a part of your everyday life. You'll be glad you did.

Also, remember, as you read, that all the information provided in this book may not be appropriate for everybody. If you have any health concerns, or any question about whether these health hints are right for you, please consult your physician prior to following the advice contained herein.

All in all, I am confident that you will find this book to be an enjoyable, educational tool that will help you lead a happier and healthier life.

—Dr. David J. Pine

1

To avoid or alleviate backaches, sleep in a fetal position with your head supported by a pillow.

2

Start your meals with a bowl of low-fat, high-protein soup. It will reduce your appetite, and you'll probably eat a smaller amount of the fattening foods that may follow. But be aware of cream-based soups—they're more fatty than most.

3

Wear a hat or cap on cool days—it will make your entire body feel warmer.

4

When you must lift heavy objects, bend your knees; do not bend at the waist.

5

Take the time to eat your meals slowly. Gulping your food is bad for digestion. If you put down your eating utensils between each bite, you will chew your food more thoroughly and enjoy it more.

6

Walk to work if you can, as walking is the most natural type of exercise. If you live too far from work to walk, try walking at lunch, or park a little farther from your office to get some extra exercise. And, step lively—a comfortably brisk pace will do you good!

7

Don't worry if you yawn a lot. Yawning is your body's natural way of increasing alertness.

8

Use sunblock every day. Even on cloudy days, the sun's harmful rays do manage to get through the clouds.

9

To prevent getting a black-and-blue mark, apply ice and pressure immediately to a potential bruise.

10

Do not take vitamins just before retiring for the night.
Your body will not digest them easily.

11

You've probably heard this a thousand times, but it
bears repeating: Use dental floss on a daily basis
for healthy teeth and gums.

12

Drink eight glasses of water every day. Water flushes out your system—sort of like an internal shower.

13

It is better for your circulation if you exercise in a cold atmosphere rather than a warm room. In this way, you maximize the exercise's impact on your cardio-vascular system.

| 14 |

When you eat omelettes, eat just the whites of the eggs mixed with broccoli, asparagus, spinach, or mushrooms for a healthful and tasty meal.

| 15 |

Dandruff problems can be significantly reduced by shampooing daily and massaging your scalp gently.

16

For dry, cracking skin on your feet, rub in petroleum jelly while your feet are still wet from a bath or shower. Then, pat your feet dry after the jelly has been applied.

17

If you own exercise equipment, make sure it is easily accessible. If it must be set up and put away each time you get the urge to exercise, chances are you won't use it much.

18

Don't eat between meals. If you feel the need to snack, choose low-fat foods, and eat sparingly. Also, try not to eat out of containers—you never know how much you're ingesting that way!

19

If you are stuck in a taxi on the way to an appointment, get out and walk instead of letting the escalating cost on the meter raise your blood pressure. You may be a little late, but you will probably be in better spirits.

20

When trying to lose weight, don't skip meals. Your blood-sugar level will drop, and you may find your-self getting grouchy.

21

Be sure to rinse packaged meats and poultry before cooking them. Don't just assume that the packing plant already did the cleaning.

22

During exercise, remember that you are not training for the Olympics. Just do as much as you feel comfortable with; exercise does *not* have to be painful to be good for you.

23

During meals, try not to eat too much in one sitting. If you skip lunch and then gorge yourself at dinner, your body ends up storing the calories you consumed as fat rather than burning them for energy as it would when digesting a smaller meal.

24

If you are in good general health and you have a choice between walking up a flight or two of stairs and taking an escalator, use the stairs for some extra exercise.

25

Don't be too quick to judge—yourself, others, or a particular situation. Being less judgmental will help reduce your level of stress.

26

If you have children, play with them! Instead of just watching them play, join them while they're jumping rope, riding a bike, or climbing on a jungle gym.

27

Always wash kitchen implements and dishes that have been in contact with raw meat before you use them for other cooking activities.

28

Breakfast is the most important meal of the day—so don't skip it! Cereal with skim milk, accompanied by a piece of fruit, is a healthy choice.

29

When exercising, make sure you stretch and warm up before starting a more intense workout. It's also a good idea to repeat your warm-up after you're done as a cool-down.

| 30 |

Don't dwell on problems that are out of your control. Stress is one of your body's greatest enemies—so avoid it!

| 31 |

Add fish to your diet. Not only is it low in fat, but it also contains agents that reduce the tendency toward blood clotting.

32

When you're outdoors, wear sunglasses that protect your eyes from ultraviolet rays.

33

Smell and examine all food carefully before eating or preparing it. Don't use items that cannot pass your own personal freshness test—no matter what the package dates say!

34

Avoid secondhand smoke. Patronize restaurants and other public facilities that offer nonsmoking sections.

35

If you are often bothered by insects, but don't like skin repellents, try rubbing a bath oil such as Avon's Skin-So-Soft on your body before going out. Studies have shown that this oil effectively repels insects (and smells a lot better than chemical sprays).

36

When you floss your teeth, do it slowly and carefully; careless flossing can hurt your teeth and gums.

37

If you find you're having trouble with your memory, try writing things down.

38

Don't exercise just before going to bed or you may have trouble falling asleep—your body needs several hours to cool down after a workout.

39

Change your socks frequently, especially in hot, humid weather. Damp feet are fertile breeding grounds for all kinds of fungi and warts.

40

If you have a lawn tractor, try pushing it instead of riding on it to take advantage of some extra exercise.

41

If you have a cat that sheds a lot, make sure you vacuum your rugs and the places where the cat sleeps on a regular basis to pick up fur and cat dander. This material can aggravate allergies.

42

During the summer, oil-free moisturizers are better for your complexion.

43

If you have a wart, avoid touching it, as this is how it will spread even further.

44

Try eating chicken and turkey hot dogs instead of those made with beef and pork. The fat content in poultry is much lower than in red meat.

| 45 |

If you feel that you may have been exposed to a sexually transmitted disease, be sure to see your doctor before having sexual contact with anyone else.

| 46 |

If you change your shampoo and conditioner to another brand every now and then, your old shampoo will work a lot better when you return to it.

47

Before you go jogging or running, be sure to do proper stretching exercises. If you don't, you may get shin splints, leg cramps, or other painful conditions.

48

If you have been given a pill prescription by your doctor, place the pills you need to take for the entire day in a pill saver box. Then you'll know exactly how many you've taken on a particular day so far, in case your memory fails you.

49

Be sensible when dieting. Any diet that promises to take off 10 pounds in a week cannot be a healthy one. Besides, when you lose weight too quickly, you gain it back just as fast.

50

Patience is a virtue—and good for you, too.

51

When baking, resist the temptation to lick the bowl! Cake batter and cookie dough both contain raw eggs—a possible health risk.

52

Wear a helmet when riding a bike or playing a contact sport. In the event of an accident, head protection could save your life!

53

A helpful hint for adding fiber to your diet: Use oats as a filler in casseroles and meat loaf.

54

Buy iodized salt. Your body needs iodine, and not many foods provide it. BUT . . . don't use an excessive amount of *any* kind of salt.

55

Aspirin interacts with other drugs, so be sure to consult a physician before taking one if you're on any prescription medication.

56

Try to eat foods in their natural states—not canned, frozen, or prepared. That's how to best take advantage of their nutritional value.

57

If you wear contact lenses, be sure to clean them faithfully each night (and according to your physician's directions).

58

If a piece of food has some mold on it, it's okay to cut around it and eat the unaffected part—but only with *solid* foods such as cheddar cheese—*not* with softer foods such as bread or jelly.

59

Steer clear of tropical oils in prepared food, and also during the cooking process. Palm kernel and coconut oil contain mostly saturated fat, which prevents your body from disposing of harmful cholesterol.

60

Use your anger constructively. Don't just suppress it—you'll end up feeling depressed or tense.

61

Hot is healthy! Hot chili peppers are great for you—if you can take the heat. They're high in vitamins A and C, have no fat, very few calories, and may act as a natural antibiotic.

62

Protect your eyes when doing yard work! Lawn-mowers and other types of outdoor equipment can fling rocks or other foreign objects at random, so be careful!

63

Eat lots of complex carbohydrates such as breads, cereal, pastas, and other grains. They give you energy-efficient fuel.

64

Don't be afraid to ask doctors and other medical personnel to wash their hands in your presence before they touch you!

65

Remember to water your plants faithfully. Some plants, such as Boston ferns, orchids, and philodendrons actually break down indoor air pollution.

66

Doctor's orders: If you have trouble remembering a doctor's advice or diagnosis, bring a relative, friend, or a tape recorder along on your visit.

67

The refrigerator is *not* the solution to your problems. Don't eat to alleviate boredom, stress, or depression.

68

Well-trimmed red meat can be leaner than chicken with the skin left on. Conclusion: An occasional portion of lean red meat will not be life-threatening.

| 69 |

Tanning salons can be bad news. They are *not* safer than sunbathing in terms of causing skin cancer. Besides, the beds pose the added risk of transmitting rashes, warts, and herpes if they are not disinfected between each session.

| 70 |

Set your limit. Decide before you get to a bar or party how much you want to drink. You don't have to leave when you reach your quota; just switch to water or soda.

71

When you're choosing a cheese, remember that the words *processed,* *product,* or *cheese food* mean it is *not* real cheese.

72

Try not to eat the same foods all the time—variety adds interest. To check your variety quotient, see how colorful the fruits and vegetables are that you've piled in your grocery cart.

73

Avoid buffet-overloading. At a buffet, it's easy to gorge yourself without realizing it. Survey the selection of dishes and choose what you want to eat, rather than trying a bit of everything.

74

To avoid blemishes, try not to touch your face. The oils in your fingertips can irritate your skin.

75

Be an active patient. Whether you are at a doctor's office or in the hospital, ask questions—information is your right!

76

Try gargling warm salt water a couple times a day to relieve a mild sore throat.

77

Just a little exercise—such as a brisk 45-minute walk five days a week—may raise your resistance to colds and flus.

78

Try taking a multivitamin daily as a supplement to a healthy diet.

79

Wash your hands before eating or applying makeup, especially if you've been around a sick person.

80

Keep a humidifier in your home to maintain moisture in the air. Dry air can irritate your nose and throat.

81

Another way to soothe a mild sore throat: Sip some hot tea with honey and lemon in it.

82

Yes, it's true: A bowl of chicken soup *can* relieve your mild cold symptoms. If you add hot pepper sauce, it will also help clear out your stuffy nose and head.

83

Make sure the shoe fits! Many corns, callouses, and bunions can be prevented by wearing shoes that fit properly.

84

When your doctor prescribes medicine for you, be sure to finish the prescription. If you stop taking the medication as soon as you feel better, you may just get sick again.

85

Try not to leave old newspapers lying around your home; molds can grow in them.

86

Always wash your hands after using the bathroom; this practice will prevent the spread of germs and bacteria.

87

When removing a splinter, make sure you sterilize the pin or needle first by soaking it in rubbing alcohol for 15 minutes, rather than holding it over a flame.

88

If you strain your back, try not to lift anything heavy for the next few days.

89

Try drinking a cup of ginger tea or ginger ale to calm a mildly upset stomach.

90

Since your feet tend to swell during the course of a day as you walk around, consider shopping for shoes in the afternoon or evening, when your feet are at their largest.

91

You can relieve mild diarrhea by eating a cup of fresh blueberries.

92

And still another way to soothe a mild sore throat: a delicious glass of apple juice!

93

If you suffer from allergies, try to keep your bathroom free of mold by removing a mildewed shower curtain and installing an exhaust fan to increase ventilation. You might also opt for a mildew-resistant paint instead of wallpaper.

94

Make an effort to expect—and accept—gradual weight loss when dieting. Shedding a pound or two in a week is not as immediately rewarding as losing ten pounds quickly, but it will probably yield longer-lasting results.

95

Add some baking soda to your bath water to relieve itching or to soothe a minor skin rash.

96

Another way to relieve a mild upset stomach: Eat a delicious banana!

97

If you have an irresistible craving for potato chips or candy, choose an individual serving size—a one-ounce bag of chips or just one candy bar (instead of a bag). If you buy a large quantity, you may find it difficult to stop eating.

98

To prevent heartburn, try standing or sitting up straight for a couple hours after eating.

99

Housework is good exercise. Scrubbing floors for an hour burns the same amount of calories as an hour of tennis-playing, so it's a practical way for busy people to get a good workout.

100

See your doctor for a complete physical at least every three years. If you are over 65 or in a high-risk category, try to see your physician at least once a year.

101

Try to avoid fruit and fruit juices, coffee, colas, and alcoholic beverages when you take aspirin or ibuprofen. These combinations may upset your stomach.

102

Hang washcloths so they can dry thoroughly instead of leaving them balled up on the side of the tub. Bacteria and mold are more likely to breed in warm, damp places.

103

Choose reduced-salt canned soups when shopping. You can always add a dash of salt if you need to—and that way, you know how much salt you're eating.

104

When selecting lettuce for a salad, try Boston lettuce instead of iceberg. As a rule, the darker the color of the vegetable, the more nutrient-rich it is.

105

If jogging a mile intimidates you, try walking a mile instead. You burn the same amount of calories—it just takes longer!

106

If you use a humidifier in your home, draining, rinsing, and drying it regularly will cut down on the possibility of the water becoming a breeding ground for bacteria, fungi, and molds.

107

Avoid taking iron-enriched vitamins with a glass of milk; milk decreases the iron's effectiveness.

108

Steam your vegetables instead of boiling them, if possible; steaming helps vegetables retain their nutrients.

109

If you use a razor with blades, replace them regularly. New blades are less likely to irritate your face or legs.

| 110 |

You can reduce your salt intake when cooking by substituting other spices such as pepper, basil, and rosemary.

| 111 |

Salad dressings that are olive oil based, as opposed to mayonnaise based, are better for you.

112

Try preparing single-dish meals, such as pasta instead of a meat-potato-vegetable combination. Most people tend to eat less if they're only served one item.

113

Avoid household bug sprays if you can, and instead, opt for an organic solution such as boric acid (which kills roaches, ants, and termites).

114

When dieting, only weigh yourself once a week. Weight usually doesn't change overnight, and it can be discouraging to check the scale all the time without seeing results. Besides, if you're exercising more, you're probably replacing your body fat with muscle, which weighs more.

115

Buy locally grown fruits and vegetables. The fresher your produce, the more vitamins it contains.

116

It's best not to cut your cuticles; they protect your fingernail beds from bacteria and infection.

117

Wear large sunglasses that cover your entire eye area. In addition to providing more protection than smaller pairs, they may help prevent wrinkles from forming around the eyes.

118

Launder your towels and washcloths frequently, especially if you or someone else in your family has been sick.

119

Avoid eating in restaurants that don't look spotless. If the dining room isn't clean, the kitchen probably isn't either—and you might get sick as a result.

120

It's a good idea to replace your cosmetics regularly because bacteria can grow in makeup over time. The more liquid the item has, the faster it needs to be replaced. Try not to use the same mascara for more than six months, lipsticks and powders for more than two years.

121

Take vacations throughout the year; a change in routine is good for your body and mind.

122

Don't forget to stand up straight. Bad posture can lead to problems such as sore muscles, backaches, and fatigue.

123

Try cutting back on the amount of chemicals you use on your lawn. They may be harmful to your family.

124

Drink a glass of warm milk at bedtime if you're having trouble falling asleep.

125

To protect yourself against harmful pesticides used on fruits and vegetables, try rinsing your hard-skinned produce thoroughly in warm water with salt and lemon juice or vinegar.

126

Try to go to sleep and wake up around the same time every day. Changing your sleep patterns can make it harder to fall asleep and wake up.

127

Wash makeup brushes and applicators once a week with warm water and dishwashing soap.

128

Keep your vegetables wrapped, and store them in the refrigerator. The more air they're exposed to, the more vitamins will escape from them.

129

When dining out, be sure your hot dishes arrive at your table *hot* and not lukewarm. Also, cold dishes need to be just that, and not room temperature. If your dishes are not served properly, this might be a clue that your meal has been sitting around for a while, and bacteria may have had a chance to grow.

130

Try to make your weekend plans significantly different from your weekday schedule. A change of pace will invigorate you and better prepare you for the upcoming week.

131

Avoid medicines that smell or look funny—for example, cracked or dull-looking capsules or liquid medicine that has particles floating in it. These may be indications that the medicine has gone bad or been tampered with.

132

If you're having trouble falling asleep, it's better not to continue tossing and turning. Instead, try reading, doing a crossword puzzle, or engaging in some activity that will distract you from your insomnia until you feel sleepy.

133

Add some asparagus to your diet. It has been shown to act as a natural diuretic.

134

Talk to your sexual partner about previous affairs. The more knowledgeable you are about the other's history, the better able you will be to protect yourself against AIDS and other sexually transmitted diseases.

135

If you're concerned about the possibility of lead in your tap water, you might want to have it tested. For more information, call Clean Water Lead Testing at (704) 251-0518.

136

Don't keep raw chicken in your fridge more than a day or two after you've bought it; it can spoil quickly.

137

It's better to remove the outer leaves of leafy vegetables such as cabbage, spinach, or lettuce; they may contain stubborn pesticide residue.

138

Try using a heavy comforter instead of an electric blanket on those cold winter nights. Electric blankets often emit high electromagnetic fields.

139

Avoid ordering hamburgers "rare." When meat is ground, any bacteria that was on the surface is spread throughout, so as a precaution, make sure ground meat is fully cooked.

140

Use a cutting board that is made of hard, nonporous wood, such as hard-rock maple. It will better resist knife grooves, where bacteria can grow.

141

When dining out, be careful about ordering un-cooked dishes such as steak tartare, sushi, and raw oysters and clams. These types of foods—as well as those containing raw eggs (such as chocolate mousse, meringue pies, and Caesar salads) can be sources of food poisoning.

142

It's true—an apple a day may reduce your cholesterol level.

143

Try alternating between white and sweet potatoes. The white variety are high in potassium, while sweet potatoes are full of beta-carotene and fiber.

144

Don't take medications in the dark, without your glasses on, or when you're sleepy. You don't want to take the wrong medication or dosage by mistake.

145

To avoid possible food poisoning, set your refrigerator to 40 degrees Fahrenheit and your freezer to 0 degrees Fahrenheit.

146

Try to keep some romance in your life. Sex is a wonderfully natural way to relax your body . . . and mind.

147

When preparing sandwiches, you might substitute mustard or horseradish for mayonnaise. These two condiments are both fat-free, act as natural antibiotics, and speed up your metabolism, causing you to burn calories more quickly. They can also help clear a stuffy head.

148

Before taking any medication, be sure the package is properly sealed, with no indication that it was opened and resealed.

149

If you feel nauseated, have some tea with ginger. Ginger is a wonderful remedy for this condition, and it can also relieve pain caused by swelling.

150

Powder your toes after a bath or shower. This practice will help your feet stay dry, and less moisture means a less hospitable place for fungus.

151

Use a thermometer while cooking. The appropriate temperature for cooked beef is 160 degrees; for fish, 140; and for poultry, 180 degrees Fahrenheit.

152

If you prefer not to take aspirin for a minor annoyance such as a toothache, try drinking some herbal tea with cloves. Cloves can relieve pain the natural way.

153

If you take bandages off blisters at night, the air will help them heal faster. Also, if a bandage covering a blister gets wet (from perspiration or bathing), replace it with a dry one.

154

Eating beans (navy, black, kidney, pinto, and lentil) on a regular basis may significantly reduce your cholesterol level and help regulate your blood-sugar level.

155

Tea fights bacteria, so substitute it for coffee on occasion.

156

Try letting internal goals such as harmony, love, laughter, and knowledge guide your decisions, as opposed to external pressures such as money, power, and success. Experts say that the more at peace you are, the slower and more gracefully you will age.

157

If you suffer from halitosis (bad breath), try brushing your tongue in addition to your teeth. Bacteria can hide there and aggravate your problem.

158

Substitute juice for soda when you're thirsty. You'll automatically cut a lot of caffeine and sugar out of your diet.

159

If your restaurant meal arrives with parsley on the side, try eating it as a healthy choice.

160

If you blow-dry your hair excessively, the heat can dry out your hair and cause it to lose its natural healthy shine.

161

Try taking several short breaks from your office activity rather than one longer break. If possible, you might put your computer printer on the other side of the room instead of right next to your desk so you'll be forced to get up and get some exercise every once in a while.

162

Use skim milk in your coffee instead of nondairy creamers, as the latter contains a lot of fat.

163

Try not to eat food right out of the container. Instead, put the amount of food you want on a plate so you're less likely to eat a whole box of cookies or a pint of ice cream without realizing it.

164

Pamper your body by taking a bubble bath or getting a massage. You will feel better about yourself, and greater self-esteem results in a healthier YOU!

165

Buy white toilet tissue instead of the colored or patterned kind. The dyes in the latter ones can irritate your skin.

166

Choose breads that are made without oil, butter, or eggs. For example, croissants and biscuits have much more fat than the average piece of whole-grain bread.

167

When you're in the sun, remember that your lips can get sunburned, too. So, use lip balms or lipsticks that contain a sunscreen.

168

Storing produce that requires humidity to stay fresh (such as celery and asparagus) in plastic bags will help them last longer.

169

Try to sit with your legs uncrossed. Crossing your legs throws your spine out of alignment, so sit up straight with your feet flat on the floor.

170

Accept your body—flaws and all—instead of forcing it to be something it's not. If you feel good about your body, you will treat it with respect, giving it the exercise, nutrition, and other pleasures it needs.

171

If you get ear infections frequently, use ear plugs when swimming or showering as a precautionary measure. Keeping ears dry can help prevent infections.

172

Be suspicious of foods that are advertised as being cholesterol-free. They may contain a lot of fat instead, and fat can raise your cholesterol level.

173

Try to avoid touching your eyes and nose—especially if you just shook someone's hand. This is how colds are spread.

174

Relieve yourself when you feel the urge, rather than holding it in until it's more convenient. Your body is trying to tell you what is best for it, so listen!

175

Include orange fruits and vegetables such as carrots, apricots, and pumpkin in your diet. They contain a high amount of beta-carotene, which boosts your immune system naturally.

176

If you keep Kosher, be careful about eating too much meat. Kosher meat is sometimes salted after the animal is slaughtered. To avoid excess salt, try taking the skin off chicken and soaking the meat in water for about an hour.

177

Make sure insect bites don't become infected by washing the affected area with soap and warm water and then applying an antiseptic.

178

Experts say that if you keep your kitchen at a cooler temperature—say, at 67 degrees instead of at 72—your canned foods will maintain their nutrients twice as long.

179

Whenever possible, try to release intense emotions that cause stress. Go ahead—laugh or cry without holding back—you'll probably feel better afterwards.

| 180 |

Treat yourself to a day at a spa, where you can be pampered from head to toe. You'll feel relaxed and at peace afterwards.

| 181 |

To keep your cholesterol consumption down, avoid egg yolks. When a recipe calls for one whole egg, you might try using two egg whites instead.

182

Very fatty foods, such as red meats or deep-fried dishes—can disrupt your immune system, so try to stay away from them.

183

Eat defrosted food within 24 hours of when it was thawed. The freezing process makes food more susceptible to bacteria once it has defrosted.

184

Choose throw rugs for your home instead of wall-to-wall carpeting. Carpeting holds mold, dust, pollen, and other health menaces. Throw rugs are more resistant to these problems, and they can be easily cleaned in a laundromat washing machine.

185

Avoid drinking alcohol while sunbathing, as you will get dehydrated faster, and you may also be more vulnerable to the sun's harmful rays.

186

Wear socks that are made of natural fibers such as cotton or wool so that sweat is easily absorbed. Dry feet are usually warm feet.

187

Thawing frozen vegetables quickly will help reduce the loss of valuable nutrients. You can thaw them out easily by putting them directly in boiling water.

188

If you are in the mood for an alcoholic beverage, opt for wine instead of beer. A glass of wine (especially one of the red varieties) can lower your cholesterol level.

189

Try not to squeeze pimples or whiteheads. In most cases, you will only aggravate the problem, and an infection may develop.

190

Think of aging as an improvement, not a problem!
Thinking young will be reflected in a healthier,
younger-looking body.

191

If you suffer from allergies, keeping both your home
and auto air-conditioned will reduce the amount of
pollen and irritants in the air.

192

Replace your toothbrush regularly to keep your teeth clean and your gums healthy, and also to prevent the virus that causes cold sores.

193

Try alternating a high-intensity workout (such as jogging or rollerblading) one day with a low-intensity workout (such as walking) the next. This schedule may encourage you to stick to your exercise plan longer.

194

Choosing cotton underwear that can breathe easily will help prevent genital health problems.

195

Substitute dates for raisins when baking if you can. Dates are high in fiber and natural aspirin and can also have a laxative effect.

196

Don't go out and party if you don't feel like it. Forcing yourself to be social when your body tells you you're not up to it can wear you out and weaken your immune system.

197

Educate yourself about your family's health history. The more you know, the better prepared you will be to take steps to prevent illnesses that you may be predisposed to.

198

Wear flip-flops when using public showers at a gym or pool. Fungi are contagious, and they breed in warm, damp places.

199

When jogging or cycling at night, wear white or bright reflective colors so that motorists can see you more easily.

200

Wash your mattress pads regularly in hot water to kill any dust mites that might be living there.

201

Reduce your susceptibility to Athlete's Foot and other fungus-related afflictions by keeping your toe-nails well groomed.

202

If your lips are chapped, try not to lick them. The soreness may be relieved temporarily, but licking will only make your lips more dehydrated as soon as the saliva dries.

203

When cooking or eating potatoes, avoid adding butter, margarine, or sour cream. Also, steer clear of french fries, which absorb the fat from the oil they're cooked in.

204

If you tend to burp a lot, avoid carbonated drinks and chewing gum. Also, try to chew your food thoroughly (with your mouth closed) before swallowing.

205

Try making your own spaghetti sauce from fresh tomatoes instead of using prepared sauces. In that way, you can control the amount of fat that goes into it.

206

When you buy new clothes, remember to wash them before wearing them for the first time. This will soften the fibers and reduce the chances of skin chafing.

207

To prevent infection, be sure to thoroughly clean any cut or scrape—no matter how minor—and apply a clean bandage.

208

Try not to use nasal decongestant sprays. They can become addictive and inhibit your nose's ability to clear itself on its own.

209

Replacing kitchen sponges frequently will help guard against food poisoning.

210

Don't let your chronological age impede your activities—age is just a number, after all.

211

If you tend to get cold sores, opt for smaller tubes of toothpaste. Every time you touch your toothbrush to the tube, you can infect the toothpaste with the virus. If you buy smaller tubes of toothpaste, you'll be forced to replace them more frequently.

212

If you give yourself an extra 15 minutes in the morning instead of rushing, you'll be more relaxed—yet less fatigued—all day.

213

Steer clear of fake nails. Experts say that press-on nails, nail extenders, and sculpted nails can all cause dermatitis and nose or eye irritation.

214

During the winter months when cold, dry weather can irritate your hands, try rubbing a thin layer of lotion on your hands at night, and then applying a second layer after a few minutes. Experts say this holds more moisture in than one heavy layer of lotion.

215

If eating beans gives you gas, try soaking your beans for 12 hours before cooking them. Experts say that this reduces the compounds in the beans that cause gas.

216

Buy tissues and toilet paper that are unscented, as fragrances can irritate the skin.

217

After a bath or shower, don't dry yourself too much. Then, while you're still damp, rub lotion over your body to keep your skin soft and supple.

218

Wear mittens instead of gloves. Keeping your fingers together will help them stay warmer, and in extreme cold, this could help guard against frostbite.

219

Turn down the brightness control on your computer screen to help reduce the strain on your eyes.

220

Since wild mushrooms can be poisonous, buy them at a store instead of picking your own.

221

Remember to clean the crevices of oft-used kitchen utensils such as can openers. Stubborn bacteria can hide there.

222

Try to rinse out your mouth after you eat. Rinsing food particles off of your teeth will help prevent plaque formation and help keep your smile bright.

223

For comfort's sake, try driving with your car seat forward, with your knees higher than your hips. You may also want to use a small pillow behind your back for additional support.

224

Don't pick at scabs. They'll fall off when they're ready to; picking at them may just increase chances of scarring or infection.

225

Cut your toenails frequently (but not too short) to help prevent ingrown toenails, which can become infected if not treated properly. And, it's better not to cut your cuticles—they protect your fingernail beds from bacteria and infection.

226

Don't forget to use a sunblock in the wintertime, even when there's snow on the ground. The sun's rays reflect off the snow and ice, so you have to be especially careful.

227

Since stinging insects seem to prefer dark colors, wear white clothing if you're going to be in an area where insects tend to congregate.

228

If you add a little vinegar to the water when preparing soup stock from bones, the vinegar may coax the calcium out of the bones and into your soup.

229

If work stress is really getting to you, but you are unable to get away physically, try a little daydreaming. Giving your mind a vacation can be an effective way to combat stress.

230

When standing, keep your weight evenly distributed over both your legs. Letting one of your hips absorb most of your body's weight may cause harmful spinal curvature.

231

As your mother probably told you: Don't slouch. Paying attention to your posture may help prevent backaches and related problems.

232

When choosing a toothbrush, opt for one with soft, round bristles. This type of brush helps to combat plaque, is less likely to wear away at your tooth enamel, and is less likely to irritate your gums.

233

Avoid wearing perfumes or colognes when you're working or playing outside. Fragrances can attract bees and wasps.

234

Wear rubber gloves when doing dishes or other types of housework. They will protect your hands from the harsh, drying effects of water and detergents, which can cause chapping.

235

If you feel nauseated, it's a good idea to drink fluids, BUT it's important to do so very slowly—sip a little bit of liquid at a time.

236

If you like to swim, opt for a pool rather than a pond or a lake, as chlorinated pools are less likely to breed bacteria.

237

If a horde of bees or wasps is following you, the best thing to do is to go indoors or jump into a pool or other body of water immediately.

238

When you brush your teeth, try holding your tooth-brush as if it were a pen. Experts say that this method is less abrasive and healthier for your gums.

239

Don't use saunas, hot tubs, or pools at health clubs (or at someone's home) if they don't look clean. If they're not cleaned regularly and properly, they can be breeding grounds for bacteria.

240

When working out at a health club, carry your own towel with you to cover the equipment before using it so you're not exposed to other people's perspiration.

241

Leave your earwax alone. Mother Nature usually knows what she's doing, so you can bet that she meant for your earwax to stay in your ear. It is a natural defense against infection and harmful moisture.

242

When traveling in foreign countries, avoid ordering your beverages "on the rocks." The ice may be made from unpurified tap water and may cause diarrhea.

243

When storing leftovers, it's better to pack warm food loosely in small containers. Large, densely packed containers of warm food take a long time to chill, which increases the risk of bacteria formation.

244

Hot baths can relieve stress! When your body is tense, the blood flow to your extremities is reduced; hot water restores circulation, and will probably make you feel much better.

245

Try to stay out of the sun between 10:00 a.m. and 2:00 p.m. (11:00 a.m. to 3:00 p.m. during Daylight Savings Time). The sun's rays are strongest and most harmful to your skin during these hours.

246

Don't make funny faces that make your eyes squint or that cause your brows to furrow. Over time, these kinds of habits can make facial wrinkles worse.

247

Try to alternate between two different pairs of athletic shoes when exercising. By doing so, your feet and legs are not subjected to the same stresses during every workout.

248

If you shop carefully, you will find that you can buy all the vitamins you need for about $10 a month!

249

Avoid eating candy and other sweets to excess, as they can contribute to high triglyceride levels.

250

When traveling, opt for sealed, carbonated beverages; they're usually safe from any harmful bacteria that could make you sick.

251

Keep your shoes on in public places to help prevent the spread of warts.

252

Remember, your doctor is not a detective; give him/her a clue to what ails you instead of projecting an "I dare you . . . find out what's wrong with me!" attitude.

253

Before attending a party, eat a snack at home so you won't be tempted by the fatty "goodies" that may be served.

254

The best way to avoid a hangover is to drink slowly, on a full stomach, in moderation.

255

If you only brush your teeth once a day, try to do it just before going to bed. And don't forget to floss!

256

Take time to pay attention to the meaningful relationships in life: your friends, spouse, children, and other relatives. Researchers say that close emotional bonds help ward off stress, high blood pressure, and other illnesses.

257

Carry your purse, briefcase (or your baby) on one side one day and the other side the following day to even out the amount of stress you place on your body.

258

The sun's rays provide your body with vitamin D, so it is important to have a lot of this vitamin in your diet if you tend to stay out of the sun for health reasons.

259

Don't wear the same pair of shoes all the time. If you alternate between different shoes, giving each pair a chance to air out, you may reduce the risk of developing warts.

260

When cycling, adjust the seat so your leg is almost straight when the pedal is at its lowest point.

261

Overeating and overdrinking can exhaust you, so keep your consumption levels down and your energy levels up!

262

When buying vitamins, keep in mind that inexpensive vitamins are just as good as those that cost two or three times as much.

263

Try not to get stuck in a rut. Making little changes in your life—such as rearranging your furniture, eating a new food, taking a different route to work—can stimulate both your body and mind.

264

Keep in mind that four ounces of wine or one ounce of liquor contains 100 calories, so try alternating alcoholic drinks with diet sodas or sparkling water.

265

Wear a broad-brimmed hat when you're out in the sunshine. Not only will it help protect your face from dangerous rays, but it will also reduce your tendency to squint, which can cause wrinkles around the eyes.

266

Avoid drinking tap water that has been sitting in plumbing pipes for too long; let the water run a little before taking a drink.

267

On long car rides, get out of the car frequently and walk around. Your back will thank you.

268

If your cuticles are dry, cracked, or cut, try applying an antibiotic cream to them. Warts, which are more difficult to treat, can enter through cut cuticles if you don't keep the area sterile.

269

If you shower at a health club, you might want to spray the shower stall with a disinfectant (such as Lysol) before getting in to prevent your chances of being exposed to harmful bacteria.

270

Tune into some tunes. Listening to music can be a wonderful way to alleviate stress.

271

When buying vitamin C, it is best to choose the kind that contains rose hips.

272

Taking a cold bath on occasion can stimulate endurance and adrenal function.

273

Try not to wear very high heels, at least not on a daily basis. They place additional stress on the balls of your feet and can strain your back.

274

Remember to use a toothpaste that has been recommended by the American Dental Association. You may not get your money's worth from a generic brand.

275

Fragrances last longer in warmer areas of the body, so it is best to apply scent to the pulse points (behind the ear, at the back of the knee, on the wrist), which tend to be warmer than other areas of the body.

276

If you are prone to snoring, don't sleep on your back. Most people snore most when lying in this position.

277

Cravings increase when you skip meals or eat erratically, so try to eat meals at the same time each day.

278

When baking, substitute wheat germ for up to half of the quantity of flour that the recipe calls for. It will give all your baked goods an extra boost of nutrition.

279

Using slow, controlled movements when exercising on machines or with weights is safer and far more effective for strengthening muscles than moving quickly.

280

If you chew a stick of sugarless gum after meals, experts say that it activates your saliva glands, which may help protect your teeth against plaque.

| 281 |

Be sure to wear your seat belt every single time you are in a moving vehicle. It is safe for pregnant women to wear seat belts—just position the lap belt beneath the abdomen. Small children always need to be fastened securely into their seat belts or car seats.

282

When staying in a hotel, reserve a nonsmoking room. Secondhand smoke—even in carpets, drapes, and furniture—is a health hazard to avoid whenever possible.

283

If heartburn is troubling you, and you have no antacids handy, drink a glass of lukewarm water, which can ease the acids back into your stomach where they belong. But avoid drinking cold water—it might make your esophagus spasm.

284

If your sinuses tend to get stuffed up, take a hot shower to clear them out. Sipping hot tea or soup will also ease the congestion.

285

If you're concerned that you're consuming too much sugar, you might want to substitute tomato (or some other) vegetable juice for fruit juices. That way, you can give your body all the same nutrients, but without the sugar.

286

If you're feeling tired, tell yourself that you can feel your second wind coming on rather than focusing on your fatigue.

287

A light-colored liquor such as white wine, beer, or vodka is less likely to give you a headache than red wine, dark rum, brandy, sherry, or scotch.

288

Try adjusting your office chair so that your knees are level with, or lower than, your hips. Doing so could help prevent back problems.

289

Writing can be a very effective way of remembering things or sorting through troubling issues, so try keeping a journal. Studies have even shown that writing reduces the number of doctor visits people make and may also boost your immune system.

290

When blowing your nose, do it gently—even if your head is very stuffed up. If you blow too hard, you may just force the mucous deeper into your sinuses or your inner ears.

291

Don't sleep with the covers pulled over your head. Doing so can deprive your head of the fresh oxygen it needs, causing you to wake up with a headache.

292

When doing things that require you to bend down low, try kneeling with one knee on a cushion, as this will put less strain on your back.

293

Make an effort to wake up at your normal time no matter when you went to sleep. Sleeping late to make up for lost sleep will only further disrupt your body's natural sleep pattern.

294

If you feel a headache coming on, you might remove your contact lenses for some immediate relief.

295

When eating meat, avoid "prime cuts," since they are heavily marbled with fat.

296

Take some time out of your schedule for yourself. Solitude can be a very therapeutic solution for alleviating the stress of your busy lifestyle.

297

If you spend a lot of time at a computer, make sure your wrists remain in a neutral position, following your arm's natural line. Finding something soft to support your wrists is also helpful.

298

Taking a 30-minute nap can be an effective way to combat fatigue and feel more refreshed and productive the rest of the day.

299

Don't feel bad about stopping a workout if you feel pain. If you ignore the pain and continue, you might end up hurting yourself.

300

Always keep in mind that it is important to read the labels on all food products.

301

Poultry, meat, and fish are more nutritious when they are baked, broiled, poached, or steamed rather than deep fried or sautéed.

302

If you work on a computer and wear glasses, make sure that your prescription takes the glare of the computer monitor into account. Let your eye doctor know what kind of work you do so he or she can best suit your needs.

303

A beverage that is very tasty but very high in saturated fat is hot cocoa made with whole milk. Try using skim milk instead.

304

When buying canned food, avoid cans with dents in them, as they might have been contaminated in some way.

305

If you're having trouble fitting exercise into your schedule, actually write it down on your calendar, and take it as seriously as you would a business appointment.

306

Although shellfish are cholesterol-rich, they do not have much effect on blood cholesterol levels when eaten in small quantities.

307

A firm mattress is much better for your back than a soft one.

308

If a tooth gets knocked out of your mouth, it is best to place it in a glass of cool milk and go to the dentist immediately.

309

Substituting margarine that is polyunsaturated for butter will make your meals more healthful.

310

To ward off fatigue when working out, try timing your breathing with your exercise.

311

A low-protein, high-carbohydrate meal may have a calming effect on you.

312

Avoid practicing the same workout routines every day, as doing so can lead to muscle imbalance and boredom.

313

Palm, coconut butter, and coconut oils are among the few vegetable derivatives that contain high concentrations of saturated fats.

:

314

It is advisable for all women to examine their breasts once a month, one week after their period ends.

315

If you are suffering from a nosebleed, try pinching the soft part of your nose for about five minutes.

316

Dressing in layers is a good defense against cold weather, as you can remove the layers when you go indoors and remain comfortable.

317

Try to increase your intake of legumes and oat bran, which are high in water-soluble fiber.

318

Your skin type determines how fragrance smells on you. The scent is stronger on oily skin because perfume floats on top of the skin. On drier skin, perfume is absorbed more quickly.

319

Fatty meals may cause you to feel sluggish, but high-protein meals will give you energy.

320

Remember that whole milk products such as cream, butter, and ice cream are high in saturated fats.

321

If you feel pain when eating extremely hot or cold foods, your teeth are hypersensitive. If left untreated, this condition can lead to tooth loss.

322

Research suggests that calcium, which we've always known is good for the bones, may also help lower your cholesterol level.

323

If you cut yourself shaving, a warm tea bag applied to the affected area can help stop the bleeding.

324

When running, keep your upper body loose and your arms close to your body. Also, try to move your arms in a straight line.

325

Wear earplugs or equivalent ear protection when using noisy tools such as power drills, lawnmowers, or vacuum cleaners. Doing so may help prevent hearing loss.

326

Install smoke detectors in your home, and replace the batteries regularly, so you'll be assured that they'll work when needed.

| 327 |

Make a point of checking sodium levels when buying prepared foods. Research indicates that three-quarters of most people's sodium intake comes from processed foods—not a salt shaker—so don't assume that just because you're not sprinkling salt on your food, you're automatically cutting sodium out of your diet.

328

Women's pants that are worn too tight can ultimately cause yeast infections and other related maladies.

329

Before handling food, don't forget to clean under your fingernails when washing your hands.

330

Many household fires start in the kitchen, so be sure to keep a fire extinguisher at hand.

331

Take your time when brushing your teeth. To really get your teeth their cleanest, brush thoroughly for two to four minutes.

332

If you smoke, try to quit. No doubt you've heard this before, but it bears repeating for the sake of your (and your family's) health.

333

Get a haircut that is flattering, but which requires low maintenance. Not only will you feel better about yourself, but the time you used to spend styling your hair can be put to more productive use!

334

When you're feeling stressed out, concentrate on dropping your shoulders to release tension.

335

You might consider calling the American Cancer Society (1-800-ACS-2345) to find out what cancer-screening tests you need and how often to get them. But, be aware that if you are in a high-risk category, you might want to be tested more frequently than is normally suggested.

336

Since there are so many breakfast cereals out on the market, why not choose one that's high in iron.

337

When starting a diet, make sure you are being motivated by your own desires and goals and not someone else's—or your weight-loss efforts may not be successful.

338

Run your tap water a minute or so in the morning to flush out contaminated water.

339

If you sit too close to the TV, you can put a strain on your eyes.

340

Varicose veins occur when the veins in the legs are not able to efficiently return blood to the heart. The best way to prevent this condition is to exercise regularly, which improves circulation.

341

Storing garlic in oil can lead to food poisoning.

342

Avoid bathing in very hot water if you have dry skin.

343

If the mucous of a cough changes from clear or white to dark green, yellow, or brown and has a foul odor, see your doctor immediately.

344

Avoid using rubber bands on your hair, as they can damage the bound area.

345

Do not cook with or drink water from the hot tap, because hot water dissolves lead more quickly.

346

Be sure to dry yourself thoroughly after bathing—especially in between your toes.

347

When using household cleaners that have strong vapors, make sure you are in a well-ventilated area.

348

Do not mix household cleaners together; the resulting fumes can be toxic.

349

Be cautious when eating raw fish, as certain varieties contain parasites.

350

When attending a cocktail party, skip the chips, cheeses, fried appetizers, and so on, in favor or raw vegetables, pretzels, boiled shrimp, and fresh fruit.

351

If your shoes push your toes together, you can get hammertoes, a very uncomfortable condition.

352

The caffeine in coffee and tea can actually make a hangover worse.

353

After swimming in chlorinated water, take a shower to remove traces of the chemical from your hair and skin.

354

Wearing high heels for eight hours can put an un-natural strain on your back and neck.

355

Hair-care products made with alcohol have a drying effect on the hair.

356

When dieting, if you lose more than two pounds a week, you are more likely to lose muscle as well.

357

Try swallowing your saliva to ease heartburn.

358

Keep nasal passages well lubricated with petroleum jelly to help avoid infections.

359

A cough, which is a healing mechanism, is the body's way of keeping the lungs and breathing passages free from dust, mucous, and infective agents. Honey is a natural expectorant that promotes the free flow of mucous.

360

Salads are great . . . but don't drown them in fatty dressings or you'll defeat your purpose in eating them.

361

Relax! When something upsets you, try to shake it off. Compulsive anger or tension throws your body off kilter.

362

Avoid drinking alcoholic beverages when taking Tylenol, as the combination can adversely affect your liver.

363

Moderate coffee drinking (two to three cups a day) is not bad for you and may even improve your thinking and your memory, but try not to drink any more than that.

364

Do something nice for someone today. You'll be amazed how good it makes you feel.

365

Wake up each day filled with optimism, positive thoughts, and bountiful energy—because this really *can* be the best day of your life!

Dr. Pine was born in Queens, New York, and was raised on the north shore of Long Island. Early interest in the health profession emerged when he was in high school, prompting him to volunteer at a Long Island hospital.

Dr. Pine continued his higher education at Vanderbilt University in Nashville, Tennessee, where he received his Bachelor of Arts degree, and then decided to go into chiropractic because of his belief in helping others maintain good health and nutrition through natural means. He graduated from the National College of Chiropractic in Lombard, Illinois, and was awarded both a Doctor of Chiropractic and a Bachelor of Science degree.

After entering into an associateship in Miramar, Florida, Dr. Pine became very active in the community, giving talks to various groups and becoming a health columnist for several local newspapers. Dr. Pine and his wife, Dale, went on to write the book, *Fitness for Couples*, which has been featured in a number of prominent magazines and talk shows.

In 1978, the doctor opened a chiropractic office in Pompano Beach, Florida, where he again offered his services to the community and the media. Currently, Dr. Pine is a local high school team physician, as well as a soccer coach, and is a member of the Broward Country Chiropractic Society, the Florida Chiropractic Association, American Chiropractic Association, ACA Council on Sports Injuries, and is a Diplomate on the National Board of Chiropractic Examiners.

We hope you enjoyed this Hay House book.
If you would like to receive a catalog featuring additional
Hay House books and products, or if you would
like information about the
Hay Foundation, please write to:

Hay House, Inc.
P.O. Box 6204
Carson, CA 90749-6204

or call:

(800) 654-5126